A New True Book

THE THIRTEEN
COLONIES

By Dennis Fradin

CHILDRENS PRESS ®

CHICAGO

First European settlers
arrive in the New York area

PHOTO CREDITS

Albany Institute of History and Art—36

The Bettmann Archive—30

Historical Pictures Service, Chicago—Cover 2, 4 (bottom left and right), 6, 7 (2 photos), 8 (right), 10, 11, 12 (2 photos), 13 (2 photos), 16, 19, 21, 22, 27 (left), 38 (left), 39, 42, 43, 44

Library of Congress—25, 41

North Wind Picture Archives—4 (top), 23, 27 (right), 29, 31, 33 (2 photos), 34, 35, 38 (right), 40

©James Rowan—8 (left)

Cover—Squanto teaching the Pilgrims how to plant corn

Library of Congress Cataloging-in-Publication Data

Fradin, Dennis B.
  The thirteen colonies.

  (A New true book)
  Includes index.
  Summary: Discusses events that led to the founding of the Thirteen Colonies.
  1. United States—History—Colonial period, ca. 1600-1775—Juvenile literature. [1. United States—History—Colonial period, ca. 1600-1775] I. Title.
  II Title: 13 colonies.
E188.F7 1988   973.2   88-11827
  ISBN 0-516-001157-X

Childrens Press®, Chicago
Copyright ©1988 by Regensteiner Publishing Enterprises, Inc.
All rights reserved. Published simultaneously in Canada.
Printed in the United States of America.
    3 4 5 6 7 8 9 10 R 98 97 96 95 94 93 92 91 90

TABLE OF CONTENTS

The Indians (above and below right) had lived in North America for thousands of years. Leif Ericsson (below left) is thought to have been the first European to explore North America about A.D. 985.

THE FIRST VISITORS
TO AMERICA

Long ago, only Indians lived in what is now the United States and Canada. Starting about the year A.D. 1000, people from Europe arrived.

At first the Europeans came just to visit. Some were explorers. Others

Fur traders came only to trade with the Indians. They did not want to take over Indian land.

were fishermen who fished the waters off the coast. Later, traders arrived. They got furs from the Indians in exchange for tools, blankets, and other items.

When they returned home, these early visitors talked about this new land.

Millions of animals, such as the moose, elk, and deer (right) roamed freely across the land. The drawing of the American Buffalo (left) was made about 1552.

America had huge forests and sparkling blue waters. It had vast stretches of rich lands. It had plenty of wildlife. And for the most part, the Indians were friendly and eager to trade.

Europeans then began to think about living in America. When a country

7

The Spaniards (right) founded Saint Augustine over 400 years ago. It is the oldest non-Indian town in the United States.

builds a settlement beyond its borders, it is called a colony. People from Spain were the first Europeans to build a colony in what is now the United States. The Spaniards founded the town of Saint Augustine, Florida, in 1565.

ENGLISH COLONISTS ARRIVE

Spain founded the first colony. But England was the main country to colonize what is now the United States.

The English built their first colony in 1585 in what is now North Carolina. This colony soon failed, and so in 1587 the English founded another colony in North Carolina.

The
baptism
of Virginia
Dare

In the summer of 1587 a
baby girl named Virginia
Dare was born. She was
the first English child born
in America.

However, when English
ships brought supplies to
this colony in 1590, they
found no people. What
happened to Virginia Dare

and the others remains a mystery. Their settlement is known as the *Lost Colony*.

In 1607 the English built Jamestown, their first American settlement that lasted. Jamestown was located in what became known as the Virginia Colony.

English settlers clear land for the Jamestown settlement, the first permanent colony in America.

The *Mayflower* (left) carried
102 Pilgrims (above).

In 1620 an English
group called the Pilgrims
came to America aboard
the *Mayflower*. The
Pilgrims built the second
English colony, called the
Plymouth Colony in what is
now Massachusetts.

Many Pilgrims died
during the first year. But

These paintings record two historic events: Squanto (left) teaching the Pilgrims to plant corn and the first Thanksgiving celebration (above).

Squanto, Massasoit, and other Indians helped the Pilgrims survive. To thank God for their survival, the Pilgrims held a celebration in fall of 1621. The Indians were invited to this feast, which became known as the first Thanksgiving.

13

Colony	1630	1660	1680	1700	1730	1760
Colonial Populations						
Total	**4,545**	**75,958**	**151,507**	**250,888**	**629,445**	**1,593,625**
Maine (counties)	400	- - - -	- - - -	- - - -	- - - -	- - - -
New Hampshire	500	1,555	2,047	4,958	10,755	89,098
Vermont	- - - -	- - - -	- - - -	- - - -	- - - -	- - - -
Massachusetts	504	22,000*	46,152*	55,941	114,116	222,600
Rhode Island	- - - -	1,539	3,017	5,894	16,950	45,471
Connecticut	- - - -	7,980	17,246	25,970	75,530	142,470
New York	350	4,936	9,880	19,107	48,594	117,198
New Jersey	- - - -	- - - -	3,400	14,010	37,510	93,819
Pennsylvania	- - - -	- - - -	680	17,950	51,707	183,703
Delaware	- - - -	540	1,005	2,470	9,170	33,250
Maryland	- - - -	8,426	17,904	29,604	91,113	162,267
Virgina	2,500	27,020	43,596	58,560	114,000	339,726
North Carolina	- - - -	1,000	5,430	10,720	30,000	110,442
South Carolina	- - - -	- - - -	1,200	5,704	30,000	94,074
Georgia	- - - -	- - - -	- - - -	- - - -	- - - -	9,578
Kentucky	- - - -	- - - -	- - - -	- - - -	- - - -	- - - -
Tennessee	- - - -	- - - -	- - - -	- - - -	- - - -	- - - -

(A dotted line means no population figures are available.)

*Figures for Plymouth are included in Massachusetts because they were combined into a single colony.

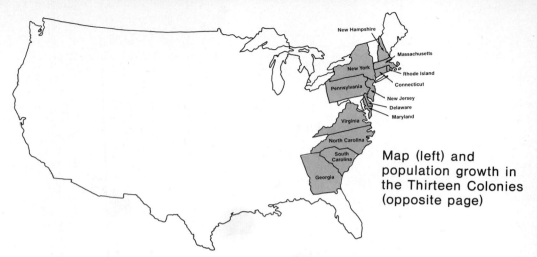

Map (left) and population growth in the Thirteen Colonies (opposite page)

England later founded or took over eleven other colonies. The eleven were New Hampshire, New York, Connecticut, Maryland, Rhode Island, Delaware, Pennsylvania, North Carolina, New Jersey, South Carolina, and Georgia. Together, these colonies became known as the Thirteen Colonies.

Of the first 1,000 colonists who came to Jamestown, all but 60 were dead by 1610.

WHY DID THE ENGLISH COME TO AMERICA?

It was difficult to survive in the new country. Many colonists starved to death during the long winters. Many others died of disease. Why, then, did

16

people come to America?

One reason was that the laws in European countries favored the oldest son. Younger sons inherited little or no land from their parents. Some of these young Englishmen came to America to get land.

A second reason had to do with religion. In England the king told people how to worship. Many people, including the Pilgrims, came to America

where they could worship
as they pleased. Rhode
Island (1636) and Pennsylvania
(1643) were havens for
religious freedom.

Some English people
came to America to teach
the Indians about
Christianity. Others came
because they thought that
America was filled with
gold and jewels! Still
others came for the
excitement of living in a
faraway land.

WHO WERE THE COLONISTS?

The Thirteen Colonies were under the rule of the kings and queens of England. Most of the colonists were English. But people from Scotland, Ireland, Germany,

The first farmhouse in Germantown

the Netherlands, France,
Sweden, and other countries
also came. These colonists
had the same reasons as
the English for coming to
America.

Some people were
brought to the colonies
against their will. They
were the black slaves from
Africa. The first slaves
were brought to Virginia
in 1619. Eventually there

The first slaves were brought to the Virginia Colony in 1619.

were black slaves in all thirteen colonies, but most lived in the South.

The colonies welcomed people of various religions. Some people belonged to the Church of England. There were Puritans and

The first church was built in New England in the early 1600s.

Quakers, Jews and Catholics, Lutherans and Presbyterians.
With all these people coming to America, the colonial population rose. By 1700 about 250,000 colonists lived in America. The first colonies—Virginia and Massachusetts—had the most people.

HOW DID THE COLONISTS LIVE?

Most of the colonists were farmers. Their first homes were small. Many families lived in log cabins, which had been first built in Delaware by

After clearing the land of trees, the family planted crops.

Swedish and Finnish settlers. Later, a farm family might build a larger wooden home. Eventually they might build a brick home—if they could afford it. In the South a few very rich families lived on huge farms called *plantations*.

The farm families grew most of their own food. They grew corn and beans. They raised hogs, chickens, and cows. Families also

A typical New England kitchen. In colonial times the kitchen was the center of most homes.

traded food with each other. Most colonists cooked their food in big pots hung over their fireplaces.

Not all the people were farmers. In the towns,

some people owned shops.
Others earned their livings
by fishing or shipping, or
by working as ministers.

Some wealthy people
bought clothes made in
Europe. But in most homes,
the women made the family's
clothes. First they spun yarn
on their spinning wheels.
Then they wove it into
cloth on their looms. After
that they sewed the cloth
into clothes.

Women spun wool into cloth on spinning wheels (left). Mothers taught their daughters how to make clothes and prepare food.

Colonial children worked
very hard. Girls helped
their mothers cook and
make clothes. Boys helped
their fathers do the heavy
farm work. Some of the

larger towns had schools,
but most children did not
go to school. Parents used
the Bible to teach their
children a little reading and
writing.

Some wealthy boys received
a fine education from tutors
or in private schools. A
few of these boys went on to
college. Among the fine
colleges founded in
colonial days were Harvard
in Massachusetts, Yale in

Harvard College was founded in 1636.

Connecticut, Dartmouth in New Hampshire, and the University of Pennsylvania.

The colonists had no movies or TV, but they found ways to have fun! Children played games similar to soccer and baseball. Horse racing was popular among adults.

Colonial women made their own candles
and many of the other things they used.

Families enjoyed Punch
and Judy (puppet) shows.
Traveling circuses went
from town to town. People
paid to see wild animals,
and to watch acrobats
swing off church steeples.
The king of England

King George III ruled the Thirteen Colonies from 1760 until the beginning of the American Revolution in 1776.

had the final say on how the colonies should be run. But the colonies also had their own governments that could decide many matters. Women, black slaves, and men who did not own property were not allowed to vote. As a result, a few rich men ran the colonial governments.

WHAT HAPPENED TO THE INDIANS?

As more and more colonists arrived, they needed more and more land. They obtained the land from the Indians, sometimes by cheating.

Angry about losing their homelands, some of the Indians fought. In March of 1622 Indians killed about 350 colonists in

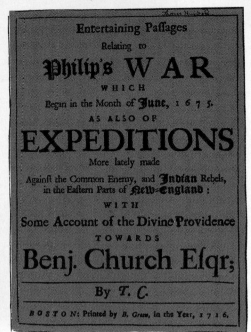

King Philip (left) and a booklet (right) published in 1716 describing the war.

Virginia. But most of the time the Indians lost their battles.

During the Pequot War of 1636-37, Connecticut's Pequot tribe was nearly wiped out. In 1675-76 an Indian named King Philip

led the Wampanoag and
Narragansett tribes against
the colonists in Massachusetts
and Rhode Island. The colonial
army nearly destroyed both
tribes in this war, which is
known as King Philip's War.

34

Some Indian tribes fought alongside the French.
They wanted to push the colonists off their land.

The Indians also fought
the colonists during the
wars that took place
between 1689 and 1763.
The wars were called the
French and Indian Wars
because the Indians joined
with the French to fight the

colonists. English soldiers helped the colonists beat the French and the Indians. After losing the French and Indian Wars, the Indians lost even more of their land.

Painting of Johnson Hall showing the Indians meeting with the colonists.

THE COLONIES BREAK AWAY FROM ENGLAND!

England needed money after the last French and Indian War in 1763. It needed money to pay for the soldiers and weapons that had helped win the war. England decided to raise the money by taxing the Thirteen Colonies. Taxes were put on sugar, paper, newspapers, tea, and many other items.

The people of Boston,
Massachusettes led the fight
against the Stamp Act.

The colonists felt that
the British government did
not have the right to tax
them. Many colonists refused
to pay these taxes. In

The Boston Tea Party (above). Americans throughout the Thirteen Colonies protested the British taxes.

December of 1773 patriots dumped a shipment of British tea into Boston Harbor. This event became known as the Boston Tea Party.

The Minutemen fought the British Redcoats at Concord.

Finally, war broke out between the colonists and the British. It began at the towns of Lexington and Concord, Massachusetts on April 19, 1775. The war for

independence is known as
the Revolutionary War, or
the American Revolution.

At the time the war
began, the colonists had
their own government called
the Continental Congress.

The first Continental
Congress met in
Carpenter's Hall in
Philadelphia,
Pennsylvania.
George Washington,
Patrick Henry, and
Alexander Hamilton
were among the
colonists who
protested British rule.

Benjamin Franklin
reads the Declaration
of Independence
written by Thomas
Jefferson (standing).

In 1776 the Congress
created the Declaration
of Independence to tell
why America was breaking
away from England.

It took more than a
piece of paper to free
America from England. The

country had to win the
Revolutionary War. For
years, the American army
led by General George
Washington seemed too
weak to win. But after the
army survived the terrible
winter of 1777-78 at
Valley Forge, Pennsylvania
things began to change.

More than
3,000 American
soldiers died
of hunger,
disease, and
cold at
Valley Forge.

General Washington accepts the British surrender at
Yorktown. Yorktown was just a few miles from where the British
had built their first settlement—Jamestown—in 1607.

In spring of 1778, France
joined with the Americans
in fighting the British. The
French helped the Americans
win the Revolutionary War.

The war's last big battle
was a great American
victory at Yorktown,
Virginia, in October of 1781.

Across America, people

John Nixon reading the Declaration of Independence to cheering citizens in the state house yard, Philadelphia, July 8, 1776

celebrated the end of the war. Bells were rung. Cannons were fired. Fireworks were shot off. The Americans were happy because the Thirteen Colonies had become the thirteen United States of America!

WORDS YOU SHOULD KNOW

Boston Tea Party (BAW • stun TEE PAR • tee) — the event in which Massachusetts patriots dumped British tea into Boston Harbor in 1773

colony (KAHL • uh • nee) — a settlement built by a country beyond its borders

Continental Congress (KAHN • tih • nen • til KAHN • gress) — the government the colonists formed in 1774, during the troubles with Britain

Declaration of Independence (deh • clair • AY • shun UV in • dih • PEN • dince) — the paper, written by Thomas Jefferson, which told why America was breaking away from Britain

Indians (IN • dyenz) — the people who lived in America before the colonists arrived

Jamestown, Virginia (JAIMZ • town ver • JIN • ya) — the first permanent English town in what is now the United States

Lost Colony (LAWST KAHL • uh • nee) — a colony built in North Carolina in 1587 that disappeared

patriots (PAY • tree • ots) — people who fight or otherwise stand up for their country

Pilgrims (PIL • grimz) — the founders of the Plymouth Colony in what is now Massachusetts

plantations (plan • TAY • shunz) — very large farms

Revolutionary War (rev • uh • LOO • shun • air • ee WAHR) (or **American Revolution**) — the war in which the Thirteen Colonies won their freedom from Britain

Saint Augustine, Florida (SAYNT AWG • us • teen FLORE • ih • dah) — the first European town built in what is now the United States; it was built by the Spanish in 1565

slaves(SLAIVZ) —people who are owned by other people

Thanksgiving(thanx•GIVE•ing) —a holiday resulting from the Pilgrims' thanksgiving celebration of 1621

Thirteen Colonies(ther•TEEN KAHL•uh•neez) —England's colonies in America; they were Virginia, Massachusetts, New Hampshire, New York, Connecticut, Maryland, Rhode Island, Delaware, Pennsylvania, North Carolina, New Jersey, South Carolina, and Georgia

tutors(TOO•terz) —private teachers

United States of America(yoo•NYTE•ed STAITZ UV ah•MAIR•ih•kah) —the country that the Thirteen Colonies became

Virginia Dare(ver•JIN•ya DAIR) —the first English child born in what is now the United States

INDEX

About the Author

Dennis Fradin attended Northwestern University on a partial creative scholarship and was graduated in 1967. His previous books include the Young People's Stories of Our States series for Childrens Press, and Bad Luck Tony *for Prentice-Hall. In the True book series Dennis has written about astronomy, farming, comets, archaeology, movies, space colonies, the space lab, explorers, and pioneers. He is married and the father of three children.*